she DARED

MALALA YOUSAFZAI

Also by Jenni L. Walsh

SHE DARED: BETHANY HAMILTON

she DARED

MALALA YOUSAFZAI

JENNI L. WALSH

Scholastic Inc.

ISBN 978-1-338-14904-3

10 9 8 7 6 5 4 3 2 1   19 20 21 22 23

Printed in the U.S.A.   40

First edition, January 2019

Book design by Maeve Norton

For persistent kiddos everywhere, especially Samantha, Alea, Chelsea, and Talia

CHAPTER 1

A DOCTOR IN THE MAKING

The marketplace was a blur of colors and motion. With her mum, Malala (pronounced Mah-lah-lah) walked amongst the sights and sounds and smells. The aromas of gasoline, fresh bread, and grilled meat filled her nose. Banners stretched from one side of the paved street to another, with words written in Urdu, the official language of the country of Pakistan. Awnings jutted out above the road. A bright red rickshaw, with one wheel in front and two wheels in the back, zoomed past a man on a motorbike, who honked loudly. More men and women scurried on foot, zigzagging between the automobiles. There was energy in the warm autumn air.

A man peddled his goods. "CDs! DVDs! Books!"

That last word caught Malala's ear. She was almost done with the Twilight series and she'd need another book soon. Reading was important to her. Education was, in general. It was in her blood. Her father was a teacher and even started Malala's school.

Chickens clucked from inside a wooden cage on a cart. Another man called, "Cumin! Turmeric!"

Her mum stopped, needing spices. Like ant-hills, the spices were piled high in varying shades—red, yellow, orange, green. One strong gust of wind could've sent the seeds and season-ings flying, coating the many stands, carts, and Malala's mum.

Malala noticed a girl of probably seventeen—around seven years older than her—plucking apricots from a great mound of fruits, stacking one after another in her basket. The girl stretched her arm, her large belly getting in the way. From the girl's young age, Malala guessed it was her first child and she hadn't been married long.

The next day at school, Malala thought about the girl from the market. Malala wondered how long ago the girl had stopped going to school so she could care for her husband. At fifteen? Sixteen? It made Malala's shoulders sag; girls should be able to finish school. But most Pakistani women's futures went in one of three directions: housewife, teacher, or doctor—with housewife being the most common.

For herself, ten-year-old Malala had already chosen the third direction: a doctor. Being a housewife was respectable; Malala saw how hard her own mum worked to care for their family.

And her father taught her how important teachers were. But Malala yearned to pursue a different path. She wanted to help people in her own way.

So Malala sat up straight in her blue uniform, thankful to be wearing it, and turned the page of her textbook, following along with her teacher at the front of the classroom. It didn't matter what subject was being taught—she loved them all—but today her teacher lectured on the parts of a plant.

Malala read in her textbook, *The roots of a plant also absorb water and nutrients that are needed for growth.*

She was in Year 4 of school, and Malala had many years of schooling ahead of her, especially in science. Science was an important pillar of a doctor's education. Her finger slid across the book as she read along, flicking her eyes between the words on the page and her teacher. Malala was in her happy place.

What Malala didn't know was that everything was about to change.

The girl in the market had stopped going to school because she chose to marry, have children, and cook for her husband. But soon, Malala would be *forced* to stop going to school, all because of an organization that called itself the Pakistani Taliban.

At first, Malala heard only gossip about a group of men who, out of nowhere, started to appear in the northwestern part of the Swat Valley, a region of Pakistan surrounded by sky-high mountains. The Swat River wound through the valley from north to south, with little villages and towns on either side. Mingora, the only city in Swat, was farther south. That was where Malala lived with her parents and two brothers.

The men hadn't come to her city yet. But soon Malala saw them on the news on TV. They were shown in the markets, in the streets, in the hills and forests of the valley. *Strange-looking*, that was Malala's first impression of them. She looked between the men on the TV and her father, comparing. Her father chose to keep his dark hair short. Theirs was long. Her father had only a mustache. Some of his friends had beards, but they were trimmed. These strange new men had long, straggly beards.

And while her father often wore a shirt and trousers, these men wore camouflage vests over their traditional shalwar kamiz (pronounced shal-war ka-meez), baggy, pajama-like pants and a long shirt.

Like so many others, Malala wasn't sure what to think of these intruders. But how could their arrival be good when they carried knives and rifles? Or when they sometimes wore stockings over their heads with holes for their eyes?

At times, they also wore turbans. While Malala's father didn't wear a turban, some men did. The intruders seemed to wear turbans only in black, though. Whispers traveled from one ear to the next, nicknaming the strange men the Black-Turbaned Brigade.

But why was this brigade in her valley? What did they want?

On their chests, they stuck black badges that promoted Sharia (pronounced Sha-ree-ah) law, the principles Malala and other Muslims followed as part of their faith.

Those words on the black badges confused Malala. She asked her father, "Aba, aren't we already loyal Muslims?" Malala studied and followed the Quran (pronounced Kor-an), the religious text of Islam. "Why would they threaten us?"

Malala would soon learn that the Black-Turbaned Brigade didn't interpret the Quran the same way as Malala or her family. The way the brigade interpreted the Quran meant they wanted to change Pakistan. Forcefully. And if they were successful, it would destroy Malala's hopes and dreams forever.

CHAPTER 2

THE BLACK-TURBANED BRIGADE

After the Black-Turbaned Brigade arrived, their leader started to make his voice—and his views—known. Right away. Throughout Swat Valley, the militants used their guns to seize control of police stations and other government buildings, and they set up an illegal radio station. A lot of people in Pakistan couldn't read or write. Many didn't have TVs. But most had radios, and they could listen. So the Black-Turbaned Brigade's leader spoke on the broadcasts, with energy in his voice. "I am an Islamic reformer. I am an interpreter of the Quran."

He went by the name Fazlullah (pronounced Fahz-loo-lah). And his illegal radio show earned him the nickname the Radio Mullah. Every night, from eight to ten, and every morning, from seven to nine, his words filled the Swat Valley. Fazlullah proclaimed he wanted people to adopt good habits and abandon the bad ones. People huddled around their radios—curious—but also eager for change because many were unhappy with the current Pakistani government.

Fazlullah banned men from shaving.

"Do as the Quran says. Trim closely the mustache and grow the beard!" he proclaimed.

Then during his radio show, he congratulated people who listened. "Mr. Tareen has kept his beard!" he announced. Fazlullah apparently didn't care, Malala realized, that this would put barbers out of work. He even insisted beauty parlors should close.

But how did Fazlullah have this type of power? This man may've led the Black-Turbaned Brigade, calling themselves the Pakistani Taliban, but he was not the prime minister of Pakistan, nor was he part of their government. So why was he trying to lead Pakistan?

The Pakistan Army sent three thousand troops to the hills and forests of Swat to try to silence Fazlullah and the Taliban. This caused fighting and fear.

At dinner one night, Malala's father shook his head, upset with everything going on. "I will not grow a beard for the Taliban," he insisted. He took a bite of chicken.

Malala poked her bread, called naan, into a sauce but didn't eat it. Even though the fighting hadn't reached her city of Mingora, she was distracted and worried about all the threats and changes. Fazlullah called these changes edicts.

Laws. And in his radio broadcasts, he would name those who didn't follow his orders. This made people gossip, "Have you heard about so-and-so?"

Malala wondered if people talked about her father. She sighed and started eating her bread. Her family sat cross-legged around a cloth on the floor. Across from her, Malala's father talked about the other edicts, in between bites. Such as how the new laws declared that people should no longer listen to music, watch movies, or dance.

The other night during the broadcast, Fazlullah had exclaimed, "These actions are sinful!" He believed that sinful acts were the reason Pakistan had an earthquake two years earlier. "Sinful actions will invite the wrath of God!" he had cried.

Malala remembered the shaking ground, the crumbling buildings, the landslides. It was scary and not something she wanted to relive.

"Is he right, Aba?" Malala asked her father. "Will there be another earthquake?"

"No, Jani," he replied, using his nickname for her. Jani meant "soul mate." "Fazlullah is only fooling people."

Malala's mum twisted her lips, then asked, "What is wrong with abandoning bad habits?" Malala thought of how their neighbor Mr. Kasi had given up chewing tobacco. "I like Fazlullah's ideas," her mum added.

Malala's mum was very holy. She prayed five times a day, though she didn't worship in a mosque. Only men were allowed in mosques. In general, men were treated differently from women, from the moment they were born.

Baby boys were celebrated. Baby girls were not.

When a male was born, rifles were fired. Dried fruits, sweets, and coins were tossed into the baby's cradle.

When Malala was born, her father insisted she should be celebrated the same as a boy. He told his friends, "I know there is something different about this child." He also gave his daughter a special name. He named her after Malalai of Maiwand.

Malalai was a great heroine. During a big battle in 1880, she ran onto the battlefield to tend to the wounded and give them water. Her men were losing. And the battle's course worsened when the flag-bearer was killed. Keeping a flag raised was important during battle. Malalai picked up the flag. She held it high. She marched forward and shouted for her army to continue to fight. The army rallied behind her and fought with renewed energy.

Sadly, Malalai didn't survive the battle, but it was because of her courage and persistence that her army was victorious.

Malala wondered what courageous things she would do in her own life. Being a doctor would mean she'd be able to help many people.

Then, one night, Fazlullah said something that stole Malala's breath. The tone of his voice was stern yet soft, almost as if he was trying to be persuasive. "Women are meant to fulfill their responsibilities in the home. Only in emergencies should they go outside."

"How will we go to market?" Malala's mum asked.

Her father deeply sighed. "He wants men to shop for their wives."

Malala scrunched her brows—as if her father would know what to purchase at the market. A man mainly worked, came home, ate, and slept. Her mum was the one who shopped, cooked, and cared for the family.

"What's more troubling," her father said, "is that he says girls should no longer go to school."

Not go to school? This made Malala panic inside. She had to know why. "Why doesn't the Taliban want girls to go to school?"

"They are scared of the pen," her father said. "They think when a child reads a book like you do, learns English like you are, or studies science like you love, then that child will become Westernized."

Westernized. Malala groaned. "What's so wrong with learning about other cultures?"

"Nothing, Jani. But they want only our religion to be taught in schools. Nothing else. And only to boys. The Radio Mullah has begun congratulating the girls who have stopped going to class."

Malala didn't want to be congratulated. She wanted to keep learning. If fact, she would. She wouldn't let this stop her from becoming a doctor.

Her mum now said, "I don't like this man anymore. How can he insist children who go to school will go to hell?" Malala's mum wasn't the only one who disliked Fazlullah's interpretation of the Quran. Others who were once open to Fazlullah's ideas now opposed him. In secret.

But Malala's father didn't want his thoughts to be secret. He wanted to be heard.

At dusk, her father often climbed the steps to their roof. Sometimes, Malala followed him up to the big, flat space. A cricket bat lay discarded on the concrete. Malala had played earlier with her two younger brothers and their friends. The game was a lot like baseball.

Her father gathered with his friends, drank tea, and talked. And talked. Politics was usually the topic. Now they also discussed what they heard on the Radio Mullah's broadcasts over the past few weeks.

Malala liked to listen to their discussions. But that night she also stared at the snowcapped mountains in the distance and daydreamed.

Malala didn't like the Taliban, their guns and threats, and their new ideas in her valley. Her beautiful valley. Malala believed she lived in the most picturesque place in the entire world. A heavenly kingdom of mountains, gushing waterfalls, and crystal-clear lakes.

She didn't want the Taliban to destroy their way of life. In less than a month, they had already caused too much unrest and fear. They already controlled many of the villages and towns outside of Mingora.

When would the Pakistan Army put an end to this?

Thankfully, she overheard her father say, "More troops are coming."

CHAPTER 3

NO MORE BOOKS

Pakistan's army arrived in their jeeps and helicopters. This time they sent ten thousand men, enough for some to go to Mingora. When they arrived, Malala was at school. Helicopter propellers whooshed in the sky. Malala's teacher stopped talking. Many people in Swat had never seen a helicopter before and all her classmates began looking around. Then they all raced outside.

Malala smiled. Across the school's courtyard, her father smiled, too. They were glad the army had sent more men. Glad that the army would, hopefully, put a stop to Fazlullah. But that night, all she heard was *bang, bang, bang*. It was the boom of cannons and machine guns. Malala's heart beat very fast and it was hard to fall asleep because of the noise, but she must've managed, because she woke to her mum telling her that school was temporarily closed.

Closed?

Malala stayed glued to their TV, watching the news, hoping for information, praying this would all be over soon. The fighting was happening farther north in the hills, but she could still hear the gunfire and blasts where she lived in the city.

Thankfully, within the month, the army had chased the Taliban out of Swat and into the mountains.

"Can we go back to school now?" Malala pleaded to her father.

He replied yes, but there was something he wasn't telling her.

"What is it?" she asked him.

"This will not last," he said, sadness in his eyes. "The Taliban will be back."

He was right.

The Taliban militants slowly reemerged from the forests. They started taking over police stations again. They established a curfew; no one was allowed outside after dark. The Radio Mullah began his broadcasts once more. If anything, the Taliban seemed more determined.

Now Fazlullah was saying only radio was allowed. No TVs. No CDs or DVDs. No computers. No more books.

Books!

Malala's jaw dropped as she watched the news. Hundreds of CD and DVD shops closed. The owners were too scared to oppose the Taliban. Fazlullah's men collected all their merchandise and created huge bonfires. Thick, black smoke plumed high in the sky.

It made her sick. And sad.

One of Malala's younger brothers asked, "Will we have to get rid of our TV?"

"No," Malala's father insisted. He glanced at the door. Taliban men would often barge into homes and take any TVs they heard. "We'll hide ours in the cupboard and keep the volume low."

Malala would hide her books, too. When she wasn't reading them, they went under her bed.

At night, Malala buried her head under her pillows to muffle the army's gunfire, shooting toward the mountains where the militants hid. With all the noise the army made, Malala didn't understand how it couldn't keep the Taliban out of her Swat Valley, or even stop Fazlullah's broadcasts. That is, until she learned that many of her neighbors were joining the Taliban. Some did so out of fear, to stop the Taliban from threatening them. When the Taliban went to people's homes and demanded money for rifles, some families were too poor. Instead, the Taliban took their sons to fight with them.

Throughout it all, Malala focused on what was important to her: getting an education so she could become a doctor and help people. She'd be courageous like Malalai of Maiwand while her country battled.

Six days a week, when she went to school, the big, black iron door to her Khushal Girls School was like a magical entrance to a world without violence. As the months went on and the fighting continued, school was Malala's refuge.

Then the unthinkable happened. The Taliban began bombing schools in the middle of the night. The first one was only twenty-four kilometers (fifteen miles) away. That was too close to home. It broke Malala's heart to think that any school could be destroyed.

One day after classes, she searched her kitchen for a snack. There was a large boom. Her whole house rattled and the fan above the window crashed to the floor.

No, she thought, petrified. So far, she'd only heard the bombings and fighting from a distance. But now, bombings had come to Mingora.

Malala was more scared than ever. Yet the more the Taliban tried to control Swat, the braver it seemed Malala's father became. He spoke out against them even more. To Malala, he said, "I will protect your freedom, Malala. Carry on with your dreams."

So Malala continued to learn, even if many of her classmates were too scared to go to school. Out of the twenty-seven in her class, only ten girls remained.

Determined, Malala snuck to school in plain clothes instead of her royal-blue uniform. She jumped at every little sound on the streets. She looked over her shoulder every few steps, carrying her books discreetly under a shawl.

Malala did everything she could to make sure no one knew where she was headed.

That would be bad.

In the neighboring country of Afghanistan, a different Taliban group also wanted to stop girls from going to school. There, they threw acid in the faces of girls who tried.

The idea should've filled Malala with terror, but it mostly made her angry. It made Malala want to stand beside her father and shout how this was wrong.

At eleven years old, Malala began giving speeches. Her father took her to a nearby press club, where she squared her shoulders, raised her chin, and protested the banning of schools. It turned out Malala was a very good speaker, much like her father. People listened to him, and it seemed that people wanted to listen to Malala, too. Her first speech was publicized across Pakistan with the title "How Dare the Taliban Take Away My Basic Right to Education?"

Afterward, in an interview, she said, "I don't understand what the Taliban are trying to do. How will someone accept our religion if you put a gun to their head and tell them to accept it?" She added confidently, "If you want people to be Muslim, show yourself to be a good Muslim first."

In another interview, she was asked, "What would you do if there comes a day when you can't go to school?"

"No." She shook her head. "This wouldn't happen."

"It could."

At the thought, Malala started to cry. But she still didn't believe it. She couldn't, not until a few months later when the Taliban announced a new decree: In January, all schools for girls were to close for winter break as they usually did—but not reopen in February.

The girls' schools were to remain closed.

Winter break was only weeks away.

Could she stop them?

Amidst the gunfire and explosions, Malala responded with more interviews and speeches, determined to voice how girls deserved to be educated as much as boys. After all, Malala read in the Quran how all people should seek knowledge, study hard, and learn the mysteries of the world.

Then two weeks before winter break—and after almost a year of the Taliban terrorizing her Swat Valley—Malala got the opportunity to tell the world what was happening in Pakistan. A radio correspondent who knew Malala's father was looking for a schoolgirl to write a diary for the BBC (British Broadcasting Corporation) about life under the Taliban.

Malala wanted to be that girl. She wanted someone to hear her words and stop her school from being closed.

CHAPTER 4

I AM AFRAID

"Writing this diary could be dangerous," the correspondent told Malala over the phone, "so we can't use your real name."

Malala sat on her bed and clutched her mum's cell phone to her ear. "A fake name?" Malala asked. "I'm just a child. Who would attack a child?"

There was a pause on the other end of the phone. Malala stared at her white walls. She didn't have much furniture in her room, only a bed and a desk.

"Okay, then," the correspondent said, "consider your father. Your diary could put him in harm's way."

Malala swallowed. The scary part was, her father already received threats from the Taliban. The Radio Mullah had spoken his name, and not in a congratulatory way. Some nights, her father slept at a friend's house to keep the Taliban away from his family, just in case. Other nights, her father didn't come home until midnight, after he was done with his many anti-Taliban groups and committees.

Malala's one-story home had a small yard in the front and another in the back. A tall stone wall surrounded it all. Within the wall was a gate with a door. On the nights when her father slept at home, she'd run outside, a shawl around her for warmth, and double-check the door's locks. In the backyard, Malala's mum had the idea to lean a ladder against the wall so her father could quickly climb the ladder and jump over the wall to the street if anyone came for him.

"Yes," Malala said to the correspondent. "I'll use a fake name."

Malala would write as Gul Makai (pronounced Gool Ma-kai), borrowing the name from a girl of great honor from a Pashtun (pronounced Pash-toon) folk story.

Pashtun was an ethnic group, composed of nearly four hundred tribes. Yousafzai (pronounced You-suf-sigh), Malala's family name, was one of the tribes.

In the story, Gul Makai falls in love with a boy named Musa Khan from a different tribe. Their love causes a war between the two tribes. But Gul Makai only wants peace. She uses the Quran to teach her elders that war is bad. Eventually, they listen and the fighting stops. Gul Makai is able to be with the boy she loves, despite being from different tribes.

Malala imagined Gul Makai must have been very frightened during all the fighting, and at the thought of losing Musa Khan. Malala was frightened, too. She was scared of the fighting. She was scared of losing her father, her family, her school, her future. Malala's first diary entry was titled "I Am Afraid."

But she wasn't sure how to put her thoughts into words. The correspondent said he'd help her. Each night, he'd call Malala and they'd talk. After, he'd write up what Malala told him and post it in both English and Urdu on the BBC website.

Malala was eager to start but also nervous. The correspondent wanted to hear a mix of her life at home and also the terror of the Taliban.

"Tell me about your day," he said, prompting her.

She held the phone tightly against her ear. "Well, there was a moment today that almost caused my heart to stop. I was walking home from school. Behind me, a man growled, 'I will kill you.' I walked faster and faster, then after a while, I looked over my shoulder. I have to do that a lot. To my relief, I saw he was talking on his mobile. He wasn't threatening me, he was threatening somebody else."

Malala heard the correspondent's shaky exhale. These types of threats were too common. "What else has been going on where you live?"

She bit her lip and thought of all the explosions. A few weeks back, they had lost electricity when the Taliban bombed the power station. For a time, they also lost access to clean water. It caused an outbreak of the disease called cholera. The hospitals overflowed and had to erect tents on the streets.

It was horrible.

To the correspondent she said, "I often have nightmares. I've had them for the past year, ever since the fighting began. I can hear the helicopter's propellers and their gunfire. I can hear the Taliban's bombs."

"And what do you do when you wake up?"

"I eat breakfast and I go to school. School is my haven, except now the Taliban says they will close it."

In ten days.

Malala's second diary entry was titled "I Have to Go to School."

A new entry was published every day or two. At school, people started talking about the diary. People started talking about it seemingly everywhere. Malala liked the praise, and she so badly wanted to shout, "It's me! I'm Gul Makai." But she remembered the correspondent's warning.

Malala had seen what the Taliban could do. They'd killed many people.

Even writing with a pen name was dangerous, but Malala was determined to speak out against the Taliban and add more entries to her diary.

On the day before winter break, Malala's sixth diary entry was published. This one was called "I May Not Go to School Again."

Malala had hoped the diary would *somehow* get *someone* to change their minds about the girls' schools remaining closed after winter break, but no one was doing anything.

Malala was devastated. So were her parents. They sacrificed a lot and worked very hard to open her father's first school. It was his dream ever since he was a boy, and it hadn't been easy. Malala's family was once very poor, and starting a school cost a lot of money. But they did it, and when the time came to get students to enroll, her father climbed up electricity poles—his arms and legs shaking because he was scared of heights—and hung banners advertising the school.

After his first school became successful, he opened more. Now he had three. An elementary school for boys and girls, a girls-only school, and a school for boys. Boys and girls over the age of ten weren't allowed to go to school together.

Now the school for girls—Malala's school—would be closed. Tomorrow. Malala would be without a classroom and her family would be without the income from the school.

A documentary filmmaker from the *New York Times* asked her father if they could record the school's last day. The night before, he came to Malala's home.

Malala and her father sat side by side on the carpet, and the documentary filmmaker focused a camera on them. Though Malala was nervous, she and her father started to tell their story. Malala wondered aloud, "How can they stop more than fifty thousand girls from going to school in the twenty-first century?"

"But you are going to stop going?" the documentary filmmaker asked.

"I have to. Otherwise my parents and the

school will be held responsible. That's what the Radio Mullah had said."

"So if you continue to get an education, the Taliban will go after your principal, your parents? More schools will be bombed?"

Malala glanced at her father, pain clear on her face. She nodded. Hundreds of schools were already demolished. "I didn't want to give in," she said. "I want to get my education and I want to become a doctor." Malala palmed her face, pressed her fingers into her eyes, and stifled her forming tears. Her father comforted her. A few moments passed before she looked into the camera again. "But they cannot fully stop me. I will continue to learn if it's at home, school, or somewhere else."

Malala's father said, "I keep hoping they'll change their mind about closing the girls' school."

He tried to turn on the radio, to see if there was any new information.

There was only static.

The Pakistan Army must've blocked the Taliban's broadcast. That night, at least.

The next morning, Malala awoke in her red-colored sheets with a heavy heart. She also woke with a camera trained on her again. "Be natural," the documentary makers told her.

That was kind of hard when they followed her everywhere. They filmed her as she brushed her teeth. They filmed her as she prayed. It's forbidden to fidget during prayer, so it was awkward to know there was a camera on her but she couldn't look at it.

In the main room, as Malala ate her breakfast of chapati bread and fried eggs, her father glanced out the windows, then threw a shawl over the camera to hide it. The Taliban wouldn't be happy if they saw the video equipment.

Though it was too dangerous to film Malala's walk to school, the camera crew joined Malala behind the walls surrounding the Khushal School.

At a special assembly, Malala screamed over the noise of helicopters, "Swat Valley!"

Classmates raised their fists into the air. "Long live!"

She repeated.

They responded.

The helicopters continued to make a loud chopping noise.

The end of the day came too quickly. Normally, school dismissed at one o'clock, but Malala and her friends stayed until three. Malala was determined that the Khushal School's bell would be the last to stop chiming.

They said goodbye.

With her right hand, Malala clasped a friend's hand. With her left, she held her friend's arm. They hugged.

"God willing, we will meet, okay?" Malala said.

Her friend replied, "God willing."

Then Malala left school, not sure if she'd ever go back.

CHAPTER 5

A SECRET SCHOOL

Malala was only eleven years old and no longer going to school. She sat on her bed, her book bag by her feet, and she cried. Malala thought of the girl from the market, only a few years older than she was; now Malala's future looked as if it'd be the same as the girl's.

It was all very frustrating. Fortunately, Malala was persistent and she had a voice, even if it was anonymous. As Gul Makai, she continued to share her stories about what was happening around her. Malala also continued to learn, even if she did so only in her bedroom.

Her father assured her, "You will go to school again."

Malala hoped he was right. Sometimes she doubted. Five more schools had been bombed. But why? The Taliban had already gotten what they wanted.

And what was the Pakistan Army doing, besides sitting in their bunkers on the hilltops? When the army descended to the streets, the Taliban always attacked back. But when the Taliban roamed the streets, there was never a Pakistani soldier in sight.

Malala wrote about it in her eighth, then ninth, entries:

"No Police in Sight"

"Army in Their Bunkers"

Malala dictated to the correspondent how many of her friends had fled the Swat Valley.

She titled that one "Very Dangerous Situation."

At dinner, she asked her father, "Will we also leave?"

"No, Jani," he said. "Swat has given us so much. In these tough days we must be strong for our valley."

Malala was relieved to stay, but she longed for her old life.

She missed their picnics at the river where the trees were heavy with pomegranates, peaches, and figs. She missed feeling proud as tourists visited her homeland. They used to come to the valley to ski. They'd stay in a big, fancy hotel. But foreigners no longer came. The hotels had been bombed.

Malala missed how Mingora used to be. The energy. The noise.

Now the streets were thin of people. Some buildings were pitted with bullet holes. Others were nothing but rubble. Malala and her friends no longer played tag or hide-and-seek in the streets.

Malala stayed on her property, behind the tall wall. It was safest there. The Radio Mullah made another warning that females were not to leave their homes.

Malala wrote about that, too.

Snow came, and as Malala always did, she chased snowflakes and formed snow bears in her small backyard. But she did so out of habit. Her heart wasn't in it. Especially on the day in February when her school normally reopened after winter vacation. This year, it did not.

Her brothers' schools reopened, though.

One of her brothers complained, saying he'd rather stay home like Malala.

"You don't realize how lucky you are!" Malala yelled.

Girls could not go to market. Girls could not go to school. Girls couldn't even leave their homes. Boys could do it all.

Malala felt trapped, even more so after their TV was stolen. Now it was harder for Malala's family to know what was going on. Through a small hole in a wall shared with their neighbors, they exchanged whispers.

Malala already knew things were grave. At night, all she heard was a barrage of bullets. Trembling, she slipped out of her bed to sleep with her father and mum. Still, Malala couldn't sleep.

Many rich families had the means to leave, and they did. Poorer families didn't have a choice but to stay. One night in his radio broadcast, Fazlullah wept. He was upset that so many people were leaving.

But what did he expect?

The nights were filled with gunfire. The days were filled with Taliban patrolling the streets. What was being done to stop this?

The army had four times the number of men as the Taliban. They had tanks, helicopters, and better weapons. And yet the Taliban seemed to be in charge.

Finally, a week after the girls' schools should have reopened, Malala's neighbor whispered something positive through their makeshift hole: The Taliban agreed to let girls go back to school.

A huge smile spread across Malala's face, until she learned more. The Taliban meant only girls up to Year 4 could attend, in the classes for both boys and girls. Malala was in Year 5, in the girls-only school.

But she wouldn't let that stop her. Her teacher wanted to teach and she wanted to learn, so she would pretend she was younger. The next morning, Malala got dressed for school. She reached for her normal uniform, then stopped herself. She didn't dare wear her favorite pink outfit either. Colorful clothes would bring too much attention to her. Instead, Malala dressed in plain clothes and snuck to school.

She did it the next day, too.

Malala did it every day that week, without the Taliban knowing. Her heart raced as she passed them on the streets, silently pleading with them not to read her mind, not to know her destination was a classroom. They looked so scary with their covered faces.

Malala's teacher told her, "The secret school is our silent protest."

Malala didn't dare write about it as Gul Makai. School was too precious to her.

But she didn't keep quiet otherwise. She continued to share other details of Gul Makai's life. And Malala continued to give interviews with her dad. Her mum would say, "Malala, hide your face when you talk to the media."

Malala never did, though; she didn't want to hide who she was. And Malala's mum never stopped her from speaking out about education. Maybe because Malala's mum never received one herself, something she now regretted. She stopped going to school at the age of six because she was the only girl in her class. All her girl cousins and friends stayed home, playing together and helping their mums. At the time, Malala's mum wanted to do the same, so she sold her books, used the money to buy candy, and never went back to school.

Malala's mum once said to her, "Don't wake up like me and realize what you missed years later."

She always encouraged Malala and her two brothers to get their education and create their own paths in life. And Malala was passionate about it during the interviews and speeches. Her father spoke with his hands, waving them wildly to make a point. Malala spoke with her eyes and a clear, strong voice.

"Education is education," she said. "Education is neither Eastern nor Western. It is human."

About a week after Malala started creeping to school, there was gunfire right outside her home. It was close, too close. She was frightened and ran to her father. He wrapped his arms around her, but said, "Shoo, Jani. It's okay. I think this gunfire is different. These gunshots are in jubilation." As when a baby boy was born, rifles were fired to celebrate.

"What's happening?" Malala asked him.

"I've heard there's to be a peace deal."

A peace deal, between the Taliban and the Pakistani government? Malala couldn't believe it. But she was grateful for it.

So were her parents. Both of them had tears in their eyes.

Could this also mean *all* girls' schools would reopen?

Could this mean all of the fear and destruction would stop?

For the first time in a long time, Malala was optimistic.

Within days, there was energy and noise in Mingora once again. Malala went to the market, and she was shocked to see the crowds. There was even a traffic jam of cars and buses. The Flying Coach passed, a brightly painted minibus with jangling chains.

Then something happened better than the busy market: The Taliban finally relented. They said all girls could return to school. But they would have to be veiled.

Normally, as part of their Pashtun heritage, Malala and her mum wore long head scarves to cover their hair and necks. With the addition of their other traditional clothing, only their faces and hands were visible.

By *veiled*, the Taliban meant they wanted girls to wear a burqa, which is an outer garment that covers the entire body, including the face. There is a semitransparent portion across the eyes, to see through.

Malala thought the burqa made walking difficult, but she'd wear it, even though it wasn't part of her heritage, if it meant she could go to school.

Malala gave interviews, sharing her excitement about the peace deal and girls' schools being reopened. One interview took place on the roof of the Taj Mahal Hotel. It was almost springtime. A cool breeze nipped at her face and hands.

"Let's talk peace, not war," she said.

Then her interview was interrupted. She learned the Taliban had killed a TV reporter.

Was the Taliban's peace deal only an illusion?

The thought of this man's death and the thought of the peace deal being a trick, only for the Taliban to get what they wanted, was sickening.

Malala wrote about it.

"Hope Smashed"

Soon after, Malala stopped dictating her diary, since the correspondent said there was not much more to say.

Somehow, the Taliban became even more barbaric.

Gunfire kept Malala up most nights.

Even though school was now allowed—nearly three weeks after classes normally began—only a few of her classmates who were still in Swat risked going.

Malala couldn't imagine leaving Mingora, let alone not going to school. Her father always said there was nothing more important than knowledge. So she kept going to class.

February turned to March. April passed. Then, in May, the Pakistan Army finally launched an operation to drive the Taliban out of Swat once and for all. But in order to do so, they wanted *everyone* to leave the valley.

The army walked the streets and between the buildings. In Mingora, the homes touched or sat close together, in varying shapes and sizes. A shack made of mud and stones was right next to a mansion. Most homes were only one story. The hospital and hotel stood the highest, at three stories.

Using megaphones, the army told the people of Mingora they had to go.

In her bedroom, Malala's head popped up from her biology textbook. Leave?

Tears filled her eyes.

Suddenly, missiles whistled through the sky. The Pakistan Army wasn't waiting to begin their attacks against the Taliban.

She ran to her father. He hugged her. "Don't worry, Malala, we will be back."

Malala shuddered, trying to collect herself and be brave.

"Now go," he said. "Pack. We must hurry, Jani."

Quickly, Malala gathered clothing into bags. She was so scattered and shaky that she packed mismatched clothes.

In her schoolbag she put *Oliver Twist* and *Romeo and Juliet*. She added many textbooks: math, physics, Urdu, English, Pashto, chemistry, biology, Islamic religious studies, and Pakistan studies.

That was all she packed: clothes and books. Her family didn't have a lot of expensive things. No jewelry. No laptops.

With two bags at her feet, Malala scanned her bedroom: her bed and desk. Her trophies and awards she'd won at school. She tried to commit every detail to memory, every crack on her white walls.

"Malala!" her father called.

It was time to go.

She remembered her grandmother once saying, "No Pashtun leaves his land of his own sweet will. Either he leaves from poverty or he leaves for love."

Now, Malala, her family, and the people of Swat were forced to leave for a third reason: the Taliban.

Malala held back tears. She felt she'd never see her home again.

CHAPTER 6

EXILED

As soon as Malala's family was packed, they rushed from their house, joining the many others who were fleeing from their homes. Mingora had a population of 175,000 people. Everyone was now something called an Internally Displaced Person. IDP for short. To Malala, it sounded like a disease.

She sat in the back of a neighbor's car, squished. Children sat on the laps of adults, and smaller children in their laps. She'd rather be in a car with only her family of five, but Malala's family didn't have a car. And in this overcrowded one, there was room for her to bring only a single bag, the one with her clothes. The textbooks and novels she'd packed so carefully had to stay behind. Before Malala left, she quickly whispered verses from the Quran to protect her precious books.

But at least Malala and her family were in a car. A motorbike passed with an entire family balancing on it. A bus was so full that people perched on the roof. It looked like people oozed from the windows. Rickshaws, mule carts, and trucks all carried IDPs and their belongings.

Many people hurried on foot, carrying whatever they could, while squinting into the sun. It was only late spring, but temperatures spiked into the 80s.

Everyone headed in the same direction. The street was jam-packed, and the Taliban watched from the tops of buildings as everyone fled. Where was the army now, when they were so quick to fire missiles earlier?

Malala didn't want to look up at the bearded faces of the Taliban. She rubbed her clammy hands against her pants. A line of sweat dripped down her back, partly because of being crammed together but also because if the Taliban wanted to attack, the entire valley was like a herd of cattle, slowly moving.

Malala's father told her, "In a few days, we'll return. Give it two to three days. Everything will be fine."

Malala hoped he was right.

They drove north out of Mingora. Soon they passed the Swat River on their left, huge cliffs on the right.

They drove for six hours, until they reached the village Malala's mum was from, where they still had relatives. She was lucky she had family to stay with. Others weren't as lucky. The majority of IDPs stayed in makeshift camps in tents, which were really tarps held up by big sticks. They had to wait in line for food and water.

Sickness broke out. There were rumors that Talibs, or members of the Taliban, were hiding amongst the tents.

The thought of it all made Malala shudder. So did the fact that her father left them to travel across Pakistan to hold press conferences and protests. He wanted to make sure the government got the Taliban out of their valley.

It was a relief to hear on the radio that the army was battling for Mingora. Hotels and buildings became bunkers and they fought hand to hand on the streets.

Malala wanted it all to be over. It had been longer than the two to three days her father had said. Much longer. A month passed. Then another. She wanted to return home. She missed her books.

On the day of Malala's twelfth birthday, no one remembered. It was very upsetting. Even without candles to blow out, she wished for peace in her valley. Why was it so hard to save her country?

Maybe Malala could help. When she was younger, she decided she'd become a doctor, but maybe there could be another role for her—a new role. Why should she be limited to one of only three futures when politics would give her a stronger voice? Hadn't her mum encouraged her to create her own path in life? Maybe Malala could become a politician.

Toward the end of the summer, her birthday wish for peace in her valley came true. After being exiled for four months, Pakistan's prime minister announced the Taliban was gone. At the news, Malala's father rejoined his family.

He was proud. Excited. Confident. "This is the day of conquering," he said. "We the peaceful people of Swat, we have won the battle with a sense of victory."

But was the Taliban truly gone from her valley? While her father used words like *conquer* and *victory*, Malala couldn't help feeling mixed emotions of relief, hope, and doubt. Already, before Malala even left to go home, she heard whispers about how the Taliban leaders escaped from the Pakistan Army.

On the car ride home with her family, that thought stayed with Malala. The Taliban leaders could still be out there. They could re-collect their power and come back. And if they did, would they come after her father? The Taliban had marked him as a wanted man, especially after he spent his four months of exile speaking out against them.

As the car approached her valley, she shook away these thoughts. Malala wanted to believe her father's words and she was so excited to return home.

They passed a sign.

WELCOME TO PARADISE

Malala grinned.

But her smile soon faded. She didn't realize

there'd be so much damage to her paradise. As they drove through villages, it was painful to see homes in ruin, cars burned to a crisp. She feared for what she'd find in Mingora. They passed one army checkpoint after another. Like birds, the Pakistani soldiers sat in nests with their machine guns on top of the tiny buildings.

Finally, Malala and her family reached the Swat River. Her father was overjoyed and began to cry at the sight of it. He tried to talk, but his voice was broken. From her seat, Malala touched her lips and gazed at the river, turning her head to keep it in her view as they drove. The crystal-clear water was so beautiful to see again. It appeared untouched by the battle.

Mingora had not gone unscathed, sadly. No one in Malala's family—not her father, her mum, or her younger brothers, even the youngest, who rarely stopped talking—spoke as they reentered their city. The Taliban had looted homes and shops, leaving a trail of glass and debris. Malala's

Malala was named after the war heroine Malalai of Maiwand.
From the moment Malala was born, her parents believed
she would also achieve great things.

When Malala was ten years old, a group calling themselves
the Pakistani Taliban invaded the Swat Valley, including the city
of Mingora, where Malala lived.

BEFORE THE TALIBAN FORCEFULLY TOOK CONTROL, MINGORA'S BAZAARS AND STREETS, LIKE THIS ONE, WERE CROWDED WITH PEOPLE. THEN THE TALIBAN BANNED DVDS, CDS, AND BOOKS, AND PROCLAIMED WOMEN SHOULDN'T LEAVE THEIR HOMES.

The Taliban were dangerous and used violence to maintain control. Malala felt safest when she was at school. The gate to her schoolyard felt like a magical entrance to a world without violence.

When the Taliban said girls could no longer go to school, Malala wanted to speak out and fight for her education. It was too dangerous to use her real name, so Malala used the pen name Gul Makai. From her bedroom, she spoke on the phone with a journalist, who posted her words for the world to see what was happening in Pakistan.

The Pakistan Army ordered the evacuation of the Swat Valley so they could battle the Taliban for control. Malala, at the age of twelve, became known as an Internally Displaced Person (IDP). She was exiled for four months before the army won back control.

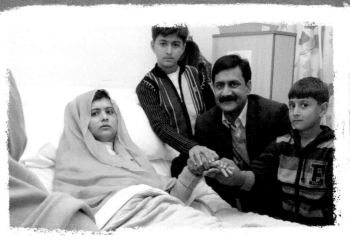

Even though the army had won, the Taliban returned when Malala was fifteen. She spoke out against them. As a way to silence Malala, they shot her. Fortunately, Malala survived the Taliban's attack and was taken to a hospital in England, where her family joined her.

Across the world, people showed their support for Malala. While recovering in the hospital, she received box-loads of letters and cards wishing her well.

AFTER LEAVING THE HOSPITAL, IT WAS TOO DANGEROUS FOR MALALA AND HER FAMILY TO RETURN TO THE SWAT VALLEY BECAUSE THE TALIBAN WERE STILL THERE. THE YOUSAFZAIS REMAINED IN ENGLAND, WHERE MALALA AND HER BROTHERS CONTINUED GOING TO SCHOOL.

Malala continued to speak out. The first speech she gave after her attack was at the Youth Takeover of the United Nations, where she spoke about the importance of education. The speech occurred on July 12, Malala's birthday, and the United Nations dubbed the date Malala Day.

FOR MALALA'S ACTIVISM, SHE WAS NOMINATED FOR ONE OF THE GREATEST INTERNATIONAL HONORS, THE NOBEL PEACE PRIZE. SHE WON, BECOMING THE YOUNGEST-EVER RECIPIENT OF THE AWARD AT THE AGE OF SEVENTEEN.

During her acceptance speech for the Nobel Peace Prize, Malala further promoted her belief that "one child, one teacher, one pen, and one book can change the world." Ironically, the Taliban's attack shined a spotlight on Malala and gave her a greater voice.

Malala has continued to spend her birthdays (and the rest of each year) fighting for education, like on this visit to Lebanon to help open an all-girls school. She has also spent Malala Days in Nigeria, Kenya, and Iraq, where she campaigned for the return of abducted girls, supported refugees, and advocated for girls' education.

eyes jumped from building to building, but she couldn't find a single one that wasn't pockmarked with bullet holes. Some buildings no longer existed at all. Green sprouts peeked out from the rubble, and weeds grew from the cracks in the pavement.

Malala's family was one of the first to brave a return. They saw no one else. The once booming, crowded city was empty. Quiet.

What would they find at their home? Malala's heart raced as they drove closer. She blew out a relieved breath when she saw, beyond the walls, the flat roof of her house still remained, then she held her breath again as her father unlocked the gate to their front yard. His words were a mixture of excitement and fear as he told his family, "Oh, my God, come on." They all entered. It was a sight to see. The trees and plants had taken over. Her front yard had become a jungle.

The first thing Malala needed to do was make sure her books were safe. She raced inside and to her bedroom. Her pink book bag was right where she'd left it. One by one she pulled free her books. Happy tears filled her eyes. She flipped through her notebooks and hugged them to her chest. Malala had always known education was important. Her parents' encouragement was unwavering. But Malala truly realized how important an education was after it was taken away, time and time again.

"When will school reopen?" she asked her father.

He wasn't sure, but he wanted to check on their schoolhouses, to make sure they weren't bombed.

Once more, Malala held her breath, letting the air out slowly when she saw that her Khushal School also still stood. The building across the street hadn't been so lucky. A missile had hit it.

Malala and her father entered the school's courtyard. Immediately he said, "Someone has been in here."

The school was dirty, with cigarette butts and empty food wrappers everywhere, and it was trashed, with desks and chairs overturned. Anti-Taliban slogans were scribbled on the walls.

Malala sighed, disappointed, because it was her army—not the Taliban invaders—who had used the school as a bunker. Why had they mistreated it?

They even used permanent marker on the whiteboards to write *Army Zindabad*.

Long live the army.

Feet dragging, Malala and her father left the school and returned home. They'd be back later to scrub the walls, to put the desks back in rows, to clean up the trash and debris.

Slowly, over the next days and weeks, others began returning to their homes.

Then, finally, after six months of being away from her school, it reopened.

CHAPTER 7

WHO IS MALALA?

When Malala finally returned to school, her life of the past two years felt like a bad dream. Every day that she sat at her desk and continued her education, she smiled. Malala progressed to Year 7, then to Year 8 and Year 9. Malala was now fifteen years old.

She studied Urdu grammar.

She wrote stories in English.

She drew diagrams of how blood circulated.

She chanted chemical equations.

She also still gave interviews.

Because the Pakistan Army still sat with machine guns in their nests on top of buildings. Why would they if the militants were gone? It had been years since the army drove the Taliban out of her valley, but after all that time, the rumors continued: The militant leaders were still free.

That left Malala feeling unsettled. She worried the Taliban could come back.

When her father gave interviews, he now questioned, "Why hasn't Fazlullah been caught?"

When Malala spoke, she stood as tall as possible to be seen and heard over the lectern, but she still felt too short behind the podium. Even though she didn't like wearing heels, she liked adding an inch or two to her five-foot height. She also liked how she felt more authoritative in the grown-up shoes.

She'd let her voice boom as she said, "I know

the importance of education because my pens and books were taken from me by force." She allowed her gaze to move from one face to another in the crowd. "But the girls of Swat are not afraid of anyone. We have continued with our education."

Malala's dedication to education was paying off. People were noticing. In 2011, Malala was one of five to be nominated for the International Children's Peace Prize, which is awarded to a child who has helped to improve the lives of children in need. She didn't win, but Malala thought the winner, Chaeli Mycroft, deserved it because Chaeli was bringing about change. At only seventeen, Chaeli had begun a campaign that fought for the rights of children with disabilities in South Africa.

Malala wanted to *do* more.

She kept speaking out. She kept fighting for education.

That same year, she was awarded Pakistan's National Youth Peace Prize. It was a big deal, not only because it was the first time Pakistan ever awarded the prize but also because Malala received it in recognition of her words as Gul Makai. Her diary was no longer anonymous. Journalists flocked to Malala's school. She nearly went blind from all the camera flashes.

People also noticed Malala's father, but it wasn't the *right* kind of people. It was people who wanted to hurt him. That became clear when he received an anonymous threatening letter. Malala assumed it was from the Taliban. They no longer went after the police and army as they had a few years ago. Now the Taliban targeted only people who spoke out against them, like Malala's father, and even Malala.

It was a scary day when Malala saw her name on the Internet. The Taliban had issued a threat against her, a fifteen-year-old girl. Malala's father went to the police. They offered Malala and her father a guard, but Malala didn't like the idea of being followed everywhere. Plus, her father thought a guard would make them more of a target.

They decided it was best if Malala kept a low profile, although Malala wasn't happy about it.

"You won't walk anywhere," Malala's mum demanded. "You'll take a rickshaw to school and you'll take the school bus home."

Malala agreed. She wanted to follow in Chaeli Mycroft's path and make a difference in the world, but she also wanted to keep her family safe.

In the mornings, Malala's father varied which of his three school buildings he went to first—the elementary school, the girls' school, or the boys'.

Before leaving home, her father looked up and down the street four or five times, searching for any signs of danger. Then he'd go.

Malala would leave next. She cut through her front yard, passing the plum and persimmon trees, and through a door in the big, metal gate. She quickly caught a rickshaw, sitting in the back as the driver took her the five-minute drive to school.

There, she slipped safely behind another big, metal gate and into her magical world without violence. Today, that magical world had an exam waiting for her. Physics. Malala liked how the subject was about principles and laws, things that couldn't be questioned. When she put her pen down, she couldn't help being annoyed, though, because she knew she'd gotten an answer wrong.

That night, Malala lay in bed, staring at the ceiling, waiting for her family to fall asleep. When all was silent, she tiptoed from window to window, making sure they were locked. She went outside, double-checking that the front gate was also locked. In her bedroom at the front of the house, she kept her curtains open. Malala wanted to be able to see everything. Recently, she'd had bad dreams where she heard footsteps behind her or saw figures slinking through the shadows.

Then Malala prayed. She said the Ayat al-Kursi, a special verse of the Quran. When said three times, her home was safe from shaya-tin (pronounced sha-yah-teen), or devils. When she said it five times, her street was safe. When she said it seven times, her neighbor-hood was protected.

Malala said it seven times, then said, "Bless us, God. First our father and family, then our street, then our whole neighborhood, then all of Swat." She paused. "No, all Muslims." She paused again. "No, not just Muslims; bless all human beings."

Normally she'd try to sleep, but since Malala was in the middle of exams, she wanted to study more.

She was still bitter about the mistake she had made during her physics exam and she needed to do better on her next test. She bit her lip. It was on Pakistan studies, a difficult subject. Malala studied until three in the morning, until she saw double—and had reread an entire textbook.

When the sun peeked over the mountains and the roosters crowed, Malala's father tried to rouse her. "Time to get up, Jani."

"A few more minutes, Aba." She added, "Please," before she pulled her quilt over her head.

He chuckled and left. Malala's mum came in next and shook her. "Pisho," she said. This meant *cat*.

Malala realized the time and remembered she had an important exam. She rushed out of bed, scrambled through her morning, and left half of her fried eggs behind.

At her desk, she took a deep breath and concentrated on the questions about the history of Pakistan's independence.

She wrote: *Pakistan became a nation when it first separated from India in 1947.* Malala added how a man named Muhammad Ali Jinnah founded Pakistan. India had both Hindus and Muslims, and Muhammad believed that Muslims should have their own nation: Pakistan.

Malala added more details and was satisfied with her answer. She moved on to the next question and the ones that followed. The exam went better than she thought it would. Her late-night studying paid off, though now she was eager to get home for an afternoon nap.

When her school bus arrived, she climbed on, yawning. The bus was actually a truck, with KHUSHAL SCHOOL painted on the side. The normal buses in Mingora were quite colorful, painted with scenes of bright pink and yellow flowers and neon-orange tigers. Dirt clung to the windows of the buses, making it hard to see in or out.

Malala's school bus didn't have windows but yellow plastic flaps, which were just as dirty as the normal bus windows. The back of the bus was open, so Malala liked to sit there to see out. She pushed her book bag under her seat, hugged her exam folder to her chest, and breathed in the stuffy autumn air.

The bus was crowded with twenty other students and three teachers. They all sat on benches, two that ran along the sides of the bus, and a third right down the middle.

Malala sat next to her best friend, Moniba. They chatted to pass the time. From the back of the bus, she watched the busyness of Haji Baba Road. Rickshaws, scooters, and pedestrians all shared the road, honking and shouting. An ice-cream boy on a red tricycle waved and Malala smiled back.

Malala saw a poster of a man with a black turban and a beard. The man was Fazlullah. In big letters under his picture, it said WANTED TERRORIST.

Despite the stuffiness and warmth of the bus, Malala shivered.

The bus groaned as it went up a hill past the snack factory. Otherwise, the normally busy and noisy road was quiet. Malala looked around, unsettled by this.

"Where are all the people?" Malala asked Moniba.

Suddenly, the driver stopped the school bus.

"Look," Moniba said. She pointed at a man approaching the bus. "It's one of those journalists. I bet he's going to ask you for an interview."

That was strange. Malala normally wasn't approached on the road, certainly not on her school bus. The man looked young, maybe the age of a college student. He wore a hat and a beard. He hopped through the open back of the bus.

"Who is Malala?" the bearded man asked.

No one replied, but Malala felt eyes on her.

The man lifted a pistol.

Malala squeezed her best friend's hand.

The bearded man fired.

CHAPTER 8

THE GIRL SHOT IN THE HEAD

The gunman fired three times. A bullet hit Malala's head, above her left eye. Two other bullets hit two of her classmates, in the hand, shoulder, and arm.

There were cries and panic.

Malala was rushed to a Swat hospital. Doctors and nurses, too many and moving too fast to count, examined her and did a scan of her head. They didn't see the bullet. Somebody stitched where the bullet hit her head and covered her forehead with a big white bandage.

Minutes later, Malala was wheeled on a gurney into an ambulance. Normal civilians injured by the Taliban were treated at the hospital, but Malala wasn't normal. She was high-profile. She was an activist. The government wanted her taken to a military hospital.

The ambulance sirens blared. Her father was with her, his eyes filled with fear for his daughter's safety and also because the Taliban could try to attack again. The helipad was only a mile away, but the drive felt as if it took forever.

Malala's father began to panic further when the helicopter wasn't yet there. Finally the helicopter landed and Malala was carried on board. Her father let out a breath and scrambled in next to his fifteen-year-old daughter.

The whooshing blades Malala had heard years ago now roared right above her. She vomited. It was scary to see blood in her vomit. Malala tried to wipe her mouth with her head scarf. Finally, they touched down at the military hospital in

Peshawar, one of the largest cities in Pakistan. Three hours after being shot, she was rushed to the intensive care unit (ICU). Malala stared blankly at clear walls surrounding her, in a space called a glass-walled isolation unit. She was restless, constantly moving her arms and legs. A nurse stilled her arm to attach an intravenous (IV) line to keep her hydrated.

Malala was examined again. "If there's an entry, there has to be an exit," a doctor mused to himself. He felt her spine, and found the bullet lodged next to her left shoulder blade.

Then, more scans of Malala's head were done. The original scan at the Swat hospital was taken only from one angle. They thought Malala's brain was fine. But the additional scans showed that the bullet went very close to her brain, splintering her skull. One of those splinters damaged the membrane around Malala's brain.

The doctor thought the best course of action was to wait and see how Malala's body reacted.

He assured Malala's father she seemed stable, but he promised to keep a close eye on her. Nurses monitored her heartbeat and vital signs. Malala was still restless. Sometimes she grunted.

Hours later, the doctor knew Malala wasn't doing well. Malala's brain was swelling. He needed to relieve the pressure.

"Surgery," the doctor told Malala's father.

Malala's eyes fluttered. She needed help.

"What will you do?" Malala's father asked.

"In order to give her brain room to expand, we need to remove a portion of her skull."

Malala's father's eyes were huge with worry. "There are risks." It wasn't a question he asked but a statement. Malala's father thought removing part of her skull sounded severe.

The doctor nodded. "The part of the brain I'll be near is very sensitive. It controls speech and Malala's right arm and leg. If things go wrong, she could be paralyzed. But if we don't perform the surgery, she could die."

Malala's father was desperate to save her. The surgery needed to be done.

To prepare, the left side of Malala's head was shaved.

The surgery took five long hours. A three-inch square of Malala's skull was removed and put into her stomach—for safekeeping. Later, after three months, they would do another operation to remove it and put the piece of her skull back in her head. For now, Malala's brain had room to heal. During the surgery, the medical team also put a tube in her neck to help her breathe and removed the bullet from her shoulder.

Afterward, Malala was put on a ventilator that blew air, through a tube, into Malala's nose.

The procedures were a success. Now they waited.

But Malala's body wasn't reacting well, even though the surgery was exactly what her body needed. Three days later, the doctors put Malala into a coma to try to help the swelling in her brain.

It was devastating for Malala's father to see her in the glass-walled cubicle, connected to many tubes. He was also very worried.

Her vital signs—Malala's body temperature, her pulse, and the rate of her breathing—weren't normal. Her face and body were swollen. Malala's organs were shutting down.

Malala had to move to another hospital for the best intensive care. The next day, she was airlifted over a hundred miles to an army hospital in another area of Pakistan.

Every major news program was covering the attack on Malala. To make matters worse, the Taliban admitted, "We did it." They also promised to finish the job.

The hospital went on immediate lockdown and the military surrounded the building with soldiers. From the roof, snipers kept watch. Not even the prime minister of Pakistan was allowed to visit Malala.

Slowly, Malala's condition improved. The doctors were hopeful that she would survive.

Malala's father cried tears of joy.

Malala's mum was finally able to join her, having a friend drive her to the hospital. It was very hard for her mum to see Malala so lifeless.

Soon, though, Malala was stable, and the doctors' thoughts turned from saving her to planning how she would recover. They didn't think her current hospital would be enough. Malala needed to be moved *again*, this time out of Pakistan. But no one in Malala's family had the proper paperwork to enter a new country. Malala's father received rushed paperwork, but he refused to leave his wife and sons in Pakistan. He thought it was too dangerous.

Malala's parents made the hard decision to have her airlifted out of Pakistan without them. It was hard for them to say goodbye.

Her father kissed her forehead and cheeks and nose. "My daughter, you are my brave daughter, my beautiful daughter," her father said over and over.

Malala woke in a medical center in Birmingham, England. She was over five thousand miles from home. It had been a week since she'd been shot.

But she didn't know any of that. In fact, Malala didn't recall a single thing from the past seven days.

The last thing Malala remembered was the bearded man boarding her school bus.

Now she was being wheeled down a hallway, flat on her back. She was alive.

Malala blinked once, twice. Her eyes felt heavy as she looked up at bright lights and unknown faces. Four faces? Eight faces? She wasn't sure. Everything was blurry. Her eyes fluttered. She was so tired. Voices floated above her, in English. Not in Pakistan's national language, Urdu.

She tried to talk, but even though she was talking in her head, no sound came out of her mouth. *Where am I?* she wondered.

Malala fought to keep her eyes open. She was scared and wanted to know what had happened. Her eyes fluttered once more, then closed.

When Malala woke again, she wasn't being wheeled down a hall. She was in a room with green walls, studying it through still-blurry eyes. There were no windows, but the room was very bright. She squinted. The room shined. It seemed very clean. The hospitals in Mingora were dirty. She wasn't in her homeland, she realized again.

Panic seized her. She had never left her country before. Where was she? Who had brought her here? Where were her father and mum? Was her father alive?

A machine monitoring her heart rate beeped wildly, matching the pounding of her heart. A man and a woman rushed to her.

The man spoke in Urdu, calming her. It was hard to hear him, as if her left ear was muted.

The woman, who wore a head scarf, took Malala's hand. "Asalaamu alaikum," she said, a traditional Muslim greeting for hello that meant "peace be unto you." She began saying prayers in Urdu and reciting verses of the Quran.

The beeping of the heart rate monitor slowed.

The woman's voice was soft. The way she spoke was soothing. Malala was still so tired.

When she woke again, Malala tried to remain calm. She breathed deeply. It felt weird. Her body hurt, especially her head. She touched her neck. A tube stuck out. Her left hand felt funny.

A nurse came in. "Are you in pain?" She spoke in English. "Blink once for *yes* and twice for *no*."

Malala blinked once. Moving her face felt funny, too.

The nurse gave Malala an injection. "For the pain," she said. Then she left. Malala waited for the medicine to help the pain in her head, but it didn't seem to do much.

Nurses kept coming in and out. A woman removed cotton from Malala's left ear. It came away bloody. She put a new one in. "You're going to be okay," Malala thought the nurse said. It was hard to hear out of that ear.

No one told her what was going on or what had happened. Malala couldn't talk to ask them questions, not with the tube in her neck. But Malala vaguely recalled the bearded man had a gun. Did he shoot her?

Finally, a nurse brought her a pencil and paper. Malala needed to ask about her father. She fumbled with the pencil. She had a hard time getting the words straight in her head. The doctor handed her a board with all the letters of the alphabet. "Spell out a word," he said.

She pointed to each letter, slowly, concentrating. Malala spelled out *father*.

"Your father is safe," he assured her.

Then where was he?

Next she spelled out *country*.

"You are in Birmingham."

She closed her eyes, trying to place it on a map. She had no idea where she was. This was so frustrating.

Malala wanted to ask more questions, but she was very tired. Her mind felt too mixed up. She was terrified. It wasn't long before sleep claimed her again.

Malala dreamed she wasn't really in a hospital. She was back on the bus, but it wasn't her best friend beside her, it was her father. The bearded man shot her. He shot her father, too. Her father disappeared. There were men everywhere. Malala searched for him, but she couldn't find him.

She woke, shaking.

Another doctor came in, a woman this time.

She gave Malala a white teddy bear. She also had a pink book with her. "Let's try this again," she said. "Can you write?"

Malala was determined. Her brow furrowed with concentration. She wrote, "Why have I no father?"

The words came out jumbled, but the doctor nodded with understanding. "Your father is safe."

The other doctor said the same thing, but Malala needed to know more. Malala pleaded with her eyes.

"He's still in Pakistan," the doctor added.

It was hard to trust their words.

She wouldn't truly believe he was safe until she saw him with her own eyes. Because if her father was fine, then why wasn't he with her? Did her parents know where she was? Maybe they were searching for her in Mingora.

It was all too much, too scary.

Later, Malala wrote *mirror* in her pink book. The woman doctor brought her one. Malala was horrified by what she saw. Her left eye bulged and was bruised. There was a scar there, too. A tube came out of her nose, another from her neck. One side of her face sagged, as if it was melting. Her lips were tilted to one side. She tried to move the left side of her face, but it was as though her brain forgot how to do that.

Instead of her normal head scarf, a white shawl draped over her head to cover her hair. She lifted it. Half her hair was gone. The rest of her hair was cut short.

She didn't look like herself. Not at all. Malala trembled.

"Hwo did this to me?" she wrote, misspelling the first word. More questions tumbled out onto the paper. "What happened to me?" she asked. "Stop lights." They were too bright. They made her head hurt.

The doctor said, "Something bad happened to you." She didn't look like she wanted to say more. So far, no one seemed to want to give her information. Maybe they were shielding her from the truth so she wouldn't be scared. Malala was already so scared. But she had to know.

"Was I shot?" she wrote. "Was my father shot?"

Malala finally received an answer. The doctor told her what happened on the school bus. Two of Malala's friends were also shot, but they were okay.

"You're very lucky," the doctor said. "The bullet could have taken out your eye or gone into your brain. But with the way you were sitting, the bullet traveled eighteen inches down to your left shoulder and stopped there. It's a miracle, really."

Malala listened intently. *So they did it*, she thought. The Taliban shot a child.

Now that she knew what happened, all she wanted was to see her parents.

She was thankful when the tube eventually came out of her throat. She didn't want her family to see her that way. Eleven days after Malala was transported to Birmingham, England, they finally arrived.

When she said hello, tears in her eyes, Malala was also thankful that her voice sounded more her own. At first, after the tube was removed, her voice had been a stranger's.

They all hugged. They all cried. It was a happy reunion. They were all safe.

"Are you okay?" her father asked. "How is your head?"

Malala lied and said it didn't hurt. She didn't want to worry her father or mum. "Did you bring my schoolbag?" she asked. Malala received some schooling at the hospital, but she knew she was falling behind.

Her parents smiled. Malala was acting like Malala.

As the weeks went on, Malala continued to improve. The first time she tried to walk, she realized her arms and legs were sluggish. Her coordination was also off and she couldn't catch a ball. She practiced until she got it right.

But Malala was still worried about her face. She couldn't move it. The doctor explained that her facial nerve had been cut. The nerve controlled how Malala opened and closed her left eye, how she moved her nose, and how she raised her left eyebrow. It also controlled her smile. Her father said he especially missed seeing her smile.

The doctor told her he'd do his best to fix the nerve. The operation took eight and a half hours. "It'll take time to see improvements," he said afterward. "Week by week, you'll have more control. But I'll need you to do facial exercises every day."

Malala eagerly agreed. The operation already helped relieve her headache. She was happy about that. Soon she was able to smile again.

Her father grinned back.

Then, nearly four months after being shot by the Taliban, Malala was ready to leave the hospital. Everyone seemed to know her story. She had received flowers, toys, pictures, and cards. Eight thousand cards in all. Many envelopes were simply addressed *Malala, Birmingham Hospital*. One even said *The Girl Shot in the Head, Birmingham*. Somehow, it ended up in Malala's hands.

People often wondered if Malala was angry.

Was she?

No.

Islam teaches humanity, equality, and forgiveness. Also, as Pashtun, Malala followed Pashtunwali, a set of moral codes. From a young age, Malala had been taught to offer hospitality, show courage, protect her honor—but also to take revenge.

Despite what had happened, Malala didn't want revenge.

Because where would *revenge* end? It could go on and on.

And also because, oddly enough, the Taliban's anger and violence ultimately gave Malala an ironic gift: a louder voice. Now the whole world knew she was fighting for education. Her campaign had become global.

Malala was only getting started.

CHAPTER 9

EDUCATION ACTIVIST

Malala ambled down the busy sidewalk in Birmingham. The air was chilly. Her mum stayed behind with her brothers. Her father walked beside her. They didn't usually make it far before she tired.

That day, Malala had Swat Valley on her mind. Her father joked that they went from being IDPs—Internally Displaced Persons—to EDPs. Externally Displaced Persons.

Malala so badly wanted to go home. It wasn't that she disliked England. In fact, she liked that the cars moved in a straight line down the street. She liked that people seemed to follow rules.

But it wasn't home. Malala and her family were staying in the center of the city, way up on the tenth floor of an apartment building with big glass windows. Nothing in Mingora had more than three stories. Outside Birmingham's town square, there were rows and rows of identical-looking houses. None of the houses in Mingora looked the same. They were higgledy-piggledy.

In the coffee shop across the street, men and women mingled. That was unthinkable in Swat. A woman was supposed to interact only with her husband or a male relative. Malala wondered what types of occupations the women lounging in the coffee shop had. Here, women held jobs beyond the three customary roles of housewife, teacher, or doctor. Girls grew up to be on the police force. They ran big companies. They could do whatever work they wanted. Women could even dress exactly as they liked.

However, Malala mused, that wasn't always a good thing. Malala never once wore anything that showed her legs. But she thought of her mum's horrified reaction the other day when she saw a group of women scurrying down the street to a bar or restaurant. Even in the dead of winter, their legs were bare, teetering on high heels.

Malala's mum cried, "Gharqa shoma!"—"I'm drowning!"

Her mum lived in purdah (pronounced purr-duh), a tradition where Muslim women don't let themselves be seen by strangers. As a result, her mum never allowed photographs of herself.

"Can we go back home soon?" Malala asked her father as they walked through the square. They passed a big fountain.

"You know we can't, Jani." It was hard to hear him over the chatter of people around them, especially with the tinny sound she heard in her left ear. "You're still getting treatments, and the schooling you are getting here is better."

What he didn't say, which Malala knew he was also thinking, was that it wasn't safe for her to return. The Taliban still wanted to silence her.

She sighed and kept walking.

School *was* better in England. There was no denying that.

In Mingora, Malala was considered "the smart girl." Her grades were always first or second best. Teachers expected more from Malala in England. She wondered if the expectations were lower in her valley because it was simply harder to go to school. Teachers were happy students were even there. It also didn't help that their science labs, libraries, and computers weren't as good back home.

Malala had a lot of catching up to do.

"Are you nervous for your operation tomorrow, Malala?" her father asked.

Malala started to say no, then stopped; a man with a beard walked toward them. Malala leaned closer to her father and held her breath. Sometimes she was convinced everyone had a gun. He passed, and Malala released her breath. She composed herself. "No."

The operation was to take the square piece of her skull from her stomach and put it back in her head. While she was in the hospital, Malala had felt the odd bump in her stomach. A nurse told her what it was. Malala found it strange they would put it there.

During her operation, it turned out that Malala's stomach didn't preserve the bone as intended. The doctors ended up not using the piece of her skull and molded a titanium plate instead. After the five-hour surgery, Malala's brain was fully protected again. The doctors also inserted an implant inside Malala's head near her ear.

A month later, they put a receiver behind her ear. Malala could hear again! Though, at first, everything in her left ear sounded robotic. It got better over time, and the annoying tinny noise was gone.

Besides still not being able to blink fully on her left side, and her left eye sometimes creeping closed on its own, Malala felt she was herself again physically.

Mentally, she was sharp. And she was ready for her words to be heard.

That next summer, she got a big chance to speak out. In fact, it was the first time she had since the Taliban's attack. Hundreds of young education advocates from around the world were invited to New York City to speak at the United Nations Youth Assembly. Malala was one of them.

At the front of the auditorium, she stood on a small box behind a podium, to give her extra height. She swallowed, nervous. *This is your chance*, she told herself.

From head to toe, she wore pink. Only her face and hands were visible. Malala rested her hands on the podium, atop her notes. And she spoke. She addressed the crowd, thanking them for having her. She also thanked everyone who helped in her recovery, even if it was only through cards and prayers. The crowd was enormous. Row after row, four hundred people sat behind long tables.

Malala referred to everyone as her dear brothers and sisters.

Her family sat in the front row. Not surprisingly, her father grinned widely. Her brothers squirmed. Her mum looked proud. She even allowed her face to be filmed for TV, a big moment.

Malala's gaze swept the large room as she spoke. Her voice was loud, clear. The cadence of her speech was slow. Malala wanted everyone to hear every word, to let her words sink in and make a difference.

"Thousands of people have been killed by the terrorists and millions have been injured," she said. "I am just one of them. So here I stand . . . one girl among many. I speak, not for myself but for all girls and boys."

Malala captivated the room.

She thought everyone should have the right to live in peace, to be treated with dignity and as an equal, and—as Malala has been saying for years—the right to be educated.

Girls shouldn't be seen differently from boys. Girls should embrace the strength within themselves. Only then will they realize their full potential.

"No one can stop us," Malala stated. "We will

speak for our rights and we will bring change through our voice. We must believe in the power and the strength of our words. Our words can change the world."

Malala believed every word that came out of her mouth.

She hoped others believed it, too. She hoped there would be change. Many clapped after she made statements. Some people had tears in their eyes.

"Let us wage a global struggle against illiteracy, poverty, and terrorism," she implored. "Let us pick up our books and pens. They are our most powerful weapons."

When she was done speaking, Malala said, "Thank you," then took a deep breath.

She received a standing ovation.

It was a special day. Malala's speech was broadcast into homes, with the caption EDUCATION ACTIVIST.

Malala liked that.

She didn't want to be thought of as the girl who was shot by the Taliban. Malala wanted to be seen as the girl who fought for education.

That day's United Nations speech was a great start. It took place on July 12, 2013, Malala's sixteenth birthday—a day the United Nations dubbed Malala Day.

Malala was already thinking what great things she could do on the Malala Days to come.

CHAPTER 10

ALWAYS PERSISTENT

Cameras flashed. The event coordinator pointed where Malala should look next. More flashes blinded her. The coordinator reminded Malala to smile. She smiled. It was a bit overwhelming, even after all the many appearances she'd done since her United Nations speech. Malala was often reminded to take a deep breath. She laughed at herself a lot, too.

When the flashes stopped, someone handed Malala a card and said, "Stay safe."

At other events, people often told her, "We are with you."

The support made Malala feel happy. It also encouraged her. Malala wanted to do more and more to promote education. She felt a great responsibility to continue her cause.

Malala met the queen of England. She met President Obama.

She won awards from America, India, France, Spain, Italy, Austria, and other countries. Then something crazy happened. She was nominated for a Nobel Prize. It was a great honor, one of the most prestigious awards recognized all over the world. Each year, Nobel Prizes are awarded to people who benefit humankind, in the categories of Physics, Chemistry, Physiology or Medicine, Literature, and Peace.

Malala's nomination was for Peace.

The Nobel Prize committee thought that all of her work contributed to increased peace between countries and the good of children and girls *everywhere*. Malala felt humbled that she received the nomination.

She also felt antsy, because it'd be months until the winners were announced.

Until then, she tried to put it out of her mind and focus on continuing her fight for education, and on her second Malala Day.

On her seventeenth birthday, she spent Malala Day in Nigeria. A few months back, militants had abducted nearly three hundred schoolgirls from their dorms in the middle of the night. These were girls who dreamed of becoming doctors, teachers, or scientists. It wasn't an easy path in Nigeria. Only four percent of girls even finished school. Malala shined a spotlight on these girls and campaigned for their safe return.

Afterward, Malala continued her own education in England, reminded once more how important education was. Three months later, she sat in chemistry class. One of her teachers called, "Malala, can I see you outside?"

Malala froze, worried. Was she in trouble? She asked, "Have I done something wrong?"

Her teacher only smiled and nodded toward the door.

In the hallway, her teacher said something unbelievable. Malala had *won* the Nobel Peace Prize.

Malala's jaw dropped, but the news didn't quite sink in. There was another winner, too, with whom she'd share the honor, a man from India named Kailash Satyarthi. He was also an activist for children's rights.

Malala thanked her teacher, but it wasn't until other teachers congratulated her, with tears in their eyes, that Malala's own eyes began to tear. The honor was sinking in.

She had won a Nobel Prize. Not only that; no one as young as Malala had ever won before. The closest to Malala's age of seventeen was Lawrence Bragg. He was twenty-five when he won—in 1915.

Right away, her school held a special assembly for her, asking Malala to speak. She did, but somehow talking to her peers was scarier than hundreds of strangers. Afterward, instead of leaving school early to celebrate, Malala immediately went to physics. She wanted to finish her school day.

On Malala's eighteenth birthday, she spent Malala Day in Lebanon. There, she opened a school for refugees who fled Syria during a civil war. The school gave two hundred teenagers an opportunity to continue their education. Many girls got married too young as a way to secure a future for themselves. Malala wanted to offer an alternative: Stay in school. With a degree, they could find work and generate an income.

On Malala's nineteenth birthday, she was in Kenya. On this Malala Day, she wanted to draw attention to the world's largest refugee camp. "I am here to speak for my unheard sisters of Somalia striving for education every day," Malala said in a speech. As in Syria, they fled during their country's civil war because it was too unsafe to stay.

On Malala's twentieth birthday, she spent Malala Day at a camp in Iraq, where people of varying beliefs and ethnicities—Iraqi, Kurdish, Yazidi, and Christian—were victimized by a terrorist group called ISIS. Over three million people were forced from their homes, half of them children. Malala offered the children encouraging words, saying, "I hope you will stay strong, go back to school as soon as you can, and have hope that your future can be better than the dark days behind you. I believe in you—and I will tell the world that you need our support."

Malala did tell the world.

She'll continue to tell the world.

Malala knows the fight for education and for

peace is ongoing. "It's hard to get things done in this world," she has said. "But you try, and you have to continue, and you never give up." Violence doesn't end through war, she believes. It is eradicated through education. She looks forward to helping on future Malala Days.

GLOSSARY

Gul Makai: the name of a brave girl from a Pashtun folk story, and the pen name that Malala used to secretly write *Diary of a Pakistani Schoolgirl*

Islam: the world's second-largest religion, which was founded by the prophet Muhammad and whose sacred book is called the Quran

Malalai of Maiwand: a hero in Afghanistan who rallied her army to victory during the 1880 Battle of Maiwand against British troops—and Malala's namesake

mosque: a Muslim place of worship

Muslim: a person who follows Islam

Nobel Prize: annual honor and prize given to people who "have conferred the greatest benefit to mankind" in the five categories of Physics, Chemistry, Physiology or Medicine, Literature, and Peace

Pashtun: an ethnic group that mainly lives in Afghanistan and Pakistan

purdah: when some Muslim women stay out of sight of men or strangers

Quran: the sacred book or scripture of Islam

RECOMMENDED READING

I Am Malala: How One Girl Stood Up for Education and Changed the World by Malala Yousafzai and Patricia McCormick

Refugee by Alan Gratz

Serafina's Promise: A Novel in Verse by Ann E. Burg

The Breadwinner Trilogy: *The Breadwinner, Parvana's Journey,* and *Mud City* by Deborah Ellis

BIBLIOGRAPHY

Books, Articles, and Videos

"Class Dismissed." Dir. Adam Ellick. *New York Times*, 2010.

"Diary of a Pakistani schoolgirl i-vi," accessed January 14, 2017, http://news.bbc.co.uk/2 /hi/7834402.stm;

http://news.bbc.co.uk/2/hi/7848138.stm;

http://news.bbc.co.uk/2/hi/7861053.stm;

http://news.bbc.co.uk/2/hi/7881255.stm;

http://news.bbc.co.uk/2/hi/7889120.stm;

http://news.bbc.co.uk/2/hi/7928752.stm

"He Named Me Malala." Dir. Davis
Guggenheim. Writer Malala Yousafzai.
Fox Searchlight Pictures, 2015.

"Malala Yousafzai's speech at the Youth Takeover
of the United Nations," accessed January 14,
2017, http://theirworld.org/explainers
/malala-yousafzais-speech-at-the-youth-take
-over-of-the-united-nations

Yousafzai, Malala, and Christina Lamb. *I Am Malala: The Girl Who Stood Up for Education and Was Shot by the Taliban*. New York: Little, Brown and Company, 2003.

Websites

NobelPrize.org, accessed January 14, 2018, https://www.nobelprize.org

Pakistani Culture, accessed January 14, 2018, retrieved from http://www.theculturalatlas.org

World Directory of Minorities and Indigenous People, accessed January 14, 2018, http://minorityrights.org/minorities/pashtuns

ABOUT THE AUTHOR

Photo by April Ziegler

JENNI L. WALSH spent a decade enticing readers as an award-winning advertising copywriter before becoming an author. Now her passion lies in transporting readers to another world, be it in historical or contemporary settings. She is a proud graduate of Villanova University and lives in the Philadelphia suburbs with her husband, daughter, son, and newfypoo. She also writes historical fiction for adults and children. Learn more about Jenni and her books at jennilwalsh.com.

Read about more girls who dared!

Don't miss:

Meet Bethany. Get inspired.